Parental Alienation Is Abuse

One Mother's Nightmare and Her Fight For Justice

Barbara Dircksen

DENVER, COLORADO

The opinions expressed in this manuscript are solely the opinions of the author and do not represent the opinions or thoughts of the publisher. The author has represented and warranted full ownership and/or legal right to publish all the materials in this book.

Parental Alienation Is Abuse
One Mother's Nightmare And Her Fight For Justice
All Rights Reserved.
Copyright © 2012 Barbara Dircksen
v2.0

Cover Photo © 2012 JupiterImages Corporation. All rights reserved - used with permission.

This book may not be reproduced, transmitted, or stored in whole or in part by any means, including graphic, electronic, or mechanical without the express written consent of the publisher except in the case of brief quotations embodied in critical articles and reviews.

Outskirts Press, Inc.
http://www.outskirtspress.com

ISBN: 978-1-4327-8984-8

Outskirts Press and the "OP" logo are trademarks belonging to Outskirts Press, Inc.

PRINTED IN THE UNITED STATES OF AMERICA

Dedication

This book is dedicated to all children and alienated parents suffering from the effects of parental alienation syndrome. Regarding my personal situation, I wrote the following poem specifically for my daughter.

Not everyone is blessed with a loving mother, if you are, that is something to forever treasure

If you're fortunate enough to have a mom so true, then you are one of the lucky few

Appreciate her with all good measure, not everyone is granted this special pleasure

Remember to treat her with kindness and grace because nobody else could take her place

Don't ever let anyone tear you apart from the love that your mother holds deep in her heart

Whatever path you take, where ever it may lead, a mother's love will always be

Book Summary

Parental Alienation is also referred to as Hostile Aggressive Parenting and it is a form of legal child abuse. It occurs when one parent undertakes a deliberate campaign to turn the child against the other and undermine the child's love for that other parent. Child custody battles are often complicated with hostile aggressive parenting, false accusations and situations where one parent alienates or brainwashes a child against the other parent with no evidence of wrongdoing. Child custody laws do not prevent hostile aggressive parenting and the most devastating cases often result in the alienation of affection toward one parent. The number of cases is steadily increasing at an alarming rate.

Does parental alienation affect you or someone you know or love? Half of all marriages end in divorce, most involving children. Approximately one third of children are born out of wedlock. Many of the parents of these children, will sometimes, act out in an unreasonable or irrational manner when dealing with their children and the other parent. Whether it is intentional or not, this causes inexcusable torment to the child by creating a constant tug-of-war between them and their parents. In an increasing number of parents, their behavior towards the opposite parent becomes so offensive that, over time, the relationship between the children and the opposite parent is eventually destroyed along with the general well-being of the child.

This is the story of how one devoted mother struggled to prevent the parental alienation that occurred between her and her beloved daughter. Her own personal account will make you realize how easy it is to become a victim of parental alienation syndrome and the devastating, long-term effects it can leave behind on the people involved.

Included at the end of this book, are some fascinating facts about Parental Alienation (PA) and Parental Alienation Syndrome (PAS) to help you discover how it may be affecting you or a loved one. Learn how to recognize the signs right from the start. Get informed and become aware. Let's all help put an end to this form of emotional abuse, known as Parental Alienation.

Contents

Introduction

One Mother's Nightmare and Her Fight for Justice 1

Conclusion..43

Parental Alienation (htt)..47

Understanding the Three Different Types of Alienation..49

Parental Alienation Syndrome is Child Abuse 69

Citation Page...73

An Excellent Source of Additional Information: 75

Introduction

Parental Alienation is a serious problem and is progressively on the rise. It is affecting millions of innocent children every day. Many more are at risk. Families that were once extraordinarily close are slowly and painfully torn apart by the continuous, deceitful brainwashing of hatred and disrespect. Valuable relationships are ruined. Its long-term effects can cause devastating feelings of guilt, hopelessness, and despair for both the targeted parent and the child.

Parental Alienation (PA) is a cruel and agonizing form of mental abuse. However, the court system rarely distinguishes it as such. This constant form of mental abuse creates havoc, not only for the targeted parent, but for the child as well. Most court officials, school personnel, and mental health professionals fail to recognize the full ramifications of this unspeakable act of contempt. This needs to change.

Parental Alienation occurs over a period of time, when

one parent continuously uses a number of brainwashing strategies in an attempt to turn their child totally against the other parent.

Parental Alienation Syndrome (PAS) is an actual condition that occurs within the child, where the child self-creates their own unjustified campaign to degrade or belittle the targeted parent. PAS is a direct result from the mental manipulation that has taken place from the alienating parent. Many times the alienating parent doesn't even realize they are putting the very happiness and well-being of their child in jeopardy. They become so consumed with bitterness and hatred that getting even with the other parent becomes their number one priority, even if it is at their child's expense.

In my particular case, the parent alienation syndrome (PAS) happened over the course of approximately six years. During that time, I have helplessly stood by as I slowly and painfully watched my loving daughter drastically transform from a gentle, caring, compassionate little girl into a hateful, rebellious, inconsiderate, disrespectful, and abusive bully. Most people probably never saw this truly obnoxious side of her the way I did because I was her main target. Through the years, her spiteful father had been continuously programming her to act out in an oppositional and hostile manner towards me, her doting, beloved mother, and it eventually sunk in. I never thought it would. It just goes to show that persistence usually does pay off in the end.

It took six years but her father had finally succeeded in turning my daughter against me. All of the never-ending brainwashing that continuously took place, day after day for six years, had taken a toll on her. She had been taught to disrespect me so badly that getting her to mind me was next to impossible. She treated me so terribly that being with her was nearly unbearable. She ultimately chose to live with her father.

I wrote this book as a way of helping me cope with the loss of my daughter, who is currently suffering from Parent Alienation Syndrome. I hope in my heart that one day, my daughter and I will reunite and regain the trust and love that we once shared. In the meantime, I am on a mission to educate and make people aware of this increasingly widespread epidemic, known as Parental Alienation Syndrome. I am willing to share private events from my personal life to give you a glimpse of what life can be like, when dealing with an alienating parent. These stories are appalling, but real. As many of you are reading this, you may find that you can relate to the horrifying series of events that eventually led to the cruel and heartbreaking alienation that took place between my daughter and I. If this is the case, know that you are not alone.

One Mother's Nightmare and Her Fight for Justice

I never imagined, in my wildest dreams that anything could ever come between me and my child, but under devious circumstances, that's exactly what happened. I have not seen or have had any contact what-so-ever with my 18 year old daughter since April 29th of 2011. We have been torn apart by lies, deception, and deceit. Nothing could have possibly prepared me for the pain, sorrow, and sheer devastation of such a spiteful and malicious act.

From the very first day my daughter was born, she had become my pride and joy; my world. She was my long, awaited baby girl; my sweet little angel from heaven above. I felt truly blessed. I was already fortunate enough to have had a son, but I've always longed for a daughter, as well.

My son was 13 years old when my daughter came

along. She was born 2 months premature and only weighed 2 lbs. 11 oz. at birth. She was so tiny and fragile and required extra care; therefore, I quit work so I'd be able to devote all my time and energy to her. I ended up being a stay-at-home mom for 12 years. By the time she was 8 months old, she developed asthma. There were countless trips to the doctor's office as well as the emergency room. Occasionally it became necessary to admit her to the hospital. I spent many sleepless nights worrying about her and taking care of her every need. I was her number one caregiver and was happy to be. I wanted the very best for my precious daughter. When it was suggested that she would most likely have developmental delays, I took her regularly to the developmental center for treatment and therapy. Eventually, as she entered into the school system, it was soon discovered that she was inflicted with learning disabilities along with ADHD. I knew that raising my daughter would not be easy but I was up for the challenge. However, I never anticipated the dreadful nightmare that lay ahead.

The relationship between her father and I became troubled shortly after my daughter's birth. Her father, who is hearing impaired, grew up with learning disabilities also. Soon after becoming pregnant with my daughter, I began to notice that her father appeared to have difficulties holding on to a job, not because he couldn't physically work, but because he had an extremely bad attitude towards people in general.

He seemed to believe that, on account of his hearing impairment, he was entitled to royal treatment. He thought everyone should have to bend over backwards for him and if they didn't, he would accuse them of discrimination. He, firmly, believed he didn't have to live up to the same expectations as everyone else. He thought he should be granted special privileges and he would demand he get them. Any time he lost a job or anything else would go wrong in his life, he would blame it on someone else and never take responsibility for his own dim-witted mistakes. He became very self-centered and was constantly claiming to be discriminated against. He thought the whole world owed him and if things didn't happen the way he wanted them to, he believed discrimination was the reason. His bad attitude got worse with every year we were together. He never could keep a job for very long. Any time he would start a new job, he would end up doing something stupid to get himself, purposely, fired. That way he could collect disability and let everyone else take care of him.

He never pitched in or helped around the house either. My daughter suffered from frequent respiratory infections since birth, due to her asthma and weak immune system. I spent much of my time taking care of a sick child, as well as handling all household chores and responsibilities, including making sure bills were paid and food was on the table. I did this on a daily basis, while also operating a childcare business out of my home to provide extra income. I honestly don't know how I ever managed it all back then. It was very difficult, but through a lot of self-determination, a great love for my daughter and by the grace of God, things always seemed to work out, somehow.

My daughter's father, on the other hand, spent most of his time on the couch, watching television. If I would ask him for any kind of help at all, he would call me a nagging bitch. He began verbally abusing me quite regularly. We separated 3 or 4 different times, but I always ended up taking him back because I couldn't trust him to take proper care of our daughter during her visits with him. After 12 long, unhappy years with him, he had become so lazy and verbally abusive that I could no longer stand it. I felt my daughter was at least old enough now to take care of herself so she didn't have to rely so much on her dad for care while staying with him. So, once again, her father and I parted ways, but this time it was permanent.

I continued providing babysitting services at the time of our final split. Within a few days after I kicked him out, I had received a call from one of the mother's I babysat for. She was quite upset because she had received a phone call from an anonymous person, saying that her kids were not safe with me because I was abusing her children. I couldn't believe my daughter's father would stoop so low as to do such a thing. I reassured the mother that I was not abusing her children. I explained the situation between my daughter's father and me. I also told her that I would totally understand if she didn't wish to continue with my childcare services any longer. I didn't want her to feel like her children were unsafe while in my care. Luckily, the next morning, she came back with the kids and apologized for doubting me. I called my daughter's father that same evening and told him that I didn't appreciate the dirty prank that he pulled, but, of course, he denied what he had done.

A few weeks later, when a custody hearing took place, he informed the lawyers and the juvenile judge that I was not a fit mother because I was abusive. Naturally, there was no evidence to support that, so it was never taken seriously, but from that point on, I realized just how bitter my daughter's father really was and that he would stop at nothing to get even with me.

He convinced himself that he could prove I was an unfit mother. He even hired a guardian ad litem to determine who would be better qualified to be awarded full custody of our daughter. Of course, he thought he should be the one. Following a short investigation, the guardian ad litem recommended to the courts that I get full custody. Even she could recognize the vast amount of hatred and contempt that my daughter's father had for me.

Since our break-up, my daughter's father has been

extremely resentful. Consequently, he has made constant attempts to turn my daughter against me, either by bad mouthing me and anyone associated with me or by buying her everything she wanted, if she would go along with his evil nonsense. He came up with some pretty outrageous lies. He would tell her things like how I was a child abuser and a slut while my boyfriend of 6 years was a sex offender and dead-beat dad and had a prison record. He didn't stop there. He also bad-mouthed just about every other family member of mine, including my daughter's older brother, whom she was very fond of. She was told that her brother was a violent drunk and he insinuated that he might hurt her in one of his drunken rages. He tried to convince her to believe that her brother was a liar and a thief and she shouldn't trust him or me. Thankfully, she was old enough and had sufficient sense to know that these sorts of statements were absolutely absurd, but, none the less, my daughter would get very upset by these continuous, derogatory remarks. She was told repeatedly what an atrocious mother I was and that I deserved to rot in jail for all the horrendous things I had done in my life. I'm sure if there was a way to actually put me behind bars, he would have found it.

On several occasions he went so far as to say, "I wish your mom and brother were dead. You'd be better off without them." When she asked her dad to stop talking so hatefully and quit making up all those outlandish lies, he would insist that they were not lies and then, punish her for taking my side. He told her that if she didn't respect his wishes, she would have all the nice things that were given to her taken away. She was basically forced to abide by his wishes or her time with him would become miserable. More times than not, she would return home, crying, because her dad's main focus during his visits with her was to bash me and my boyfriend, as well as others in my family, the entire time.

I totally despised the tremendous amount of brainwashing that her father kept forcing into her head but I could not make him understand how damaging it was for her well-being. He refused to listen to me. The more we argued about it, the more relentless he would become. I knew he was treading on a destructive path, but I was powerless to stop him.

It just so happened, my boyfriend had developed a very good relationship with my daughter. She clearly loved him like a father and this infuriated her father. She was told that she was forbidden to get too close or have anything to do with my boyfriend ever. She was not permitted to give him hugs and she was not allowed to tell him that she loved him. If he would find out about it, she would be punished. She usually ignored his ridiculous requests and enjoyed her time with me and my boyfriend anyway; she just had to keep it a secret from her dad.

He also kept reinforcing the notion that I, as her mother, was crazy and never knew what I was doing; therefore, she didn't have to listen to me. He constantly drilled into her head, over and over, that she didn't have to mind me or my boyfriend. It was only important that she listen to him because he loved her more than we did and he knew what was best for her. Furthermore, if she didn't respect his wishes, then, that would be showing disrespect for him and that would result in a punishment for her.

This was a cruel, malicious, and spiteful form of abuse on her father's part. There was a powerful tug-of-war taking place and my daughter was entrapped right in the middle, being forcefully pulled one way and then the other. On her father's side, she was being told to disrespect me and my boyfriend and then, was punished when not doing so. On the opposite side, she was expected to show respect and was punished, accordingly, if she didn't. Looking back, I cringe every time I try to imagine the pain and agony that was surely inflicted upon my daughter by this never-ending process. It had to be pure torture. I can recall how my daughter used to cry her eyes out each time her father and I had an argument. She absolutely hated the thought of us not getting along with one another. It simply broke her heart.

Many times, during her visitations with him, he would attempt to get my daughter to feel sorry for him. Once, he told her that he needed her so much more than I did and he positively could not live without her. She was told that if she favored her mom over him, he would have to kill himself. When my daughter returned home, she cried for days because she was so worried that her dad would actually do it. He was constantly trying to make her feel like he couldn't live without her by his side at all times.

In due time, her father bought my daughter a cell phone, so that he was able to contact her every day. He would call or text her several times, daily, always asking her what my boyfriend and I were doing. He never referred to us by our actual names. He only used highly offensive names, some of which were so vulgar, they weren't even suitable for a child to see or hear. Each time he contacted her, he never failed to mention what terrible parents we were or how she would be better off with him. He would continually ridicule and undermine everything we did or said. She asked him, repeatedly, to stop his hateful behavior, but he refused.

He also got himself a P.O. Box at the local post office in my hometown. That way he had an excuse to drive past my house regularly to spy on us. I would spot his vehicle driving by often. Frequently, I would notice his vehicle being parked nearby. It made me uneasy because I didn't trust him or what he might be capable of doing.

PARENTAL ALIENATION IS ABUSE

Court officials were of no help to me or my daughter. I tried to make them understand how detrimental her father's derogatory conduct was to my child. There were numerous times she didn't even want to go with her dad for visitation and she would beg me to not make her go with him. However, I was instructed by my lawyer that I had to make her go with him no matter what, even if I had to force her into his vehicle. Otherwise, I would be in contempt of court. I was told that I couldn't control how her father acts during his visitation with her. He was still entitled to see his daughter and I would simply have to accept it. It was a no-win situation.

There were many times I've had to send her with her dad, in tears, because she was forced to put up with his constant mocking of me and my boyfriend. She absolutely detested it.

I don't think that my daughter fully understood why I had to make her go with him even though she often didn't want to go. I believe she was disappointed in me because I couldn't protect her from her father's wicked ways. I felt utterly helpless. Needless to say, this viscous cycle went on for years. After a while, it became somewhat of a game which she became accustomed to.

My daughter had been seeing various different mental health officials since she was 12 to help her and me deal with her father's behavior problems and hers. Initially, her father's steady stream of brainwashing strategies didn't appear to be having too much of a major impact on her. We were both well aware that her father most likely was never going to change so we tried to ignore his bad behaviors the best we could. It was never easy. However, after a year or so following the separation, my daughter, slowly but steadily, began to show a whole other side of herself. She was becoming hateful, obnoxious, and extremely defiant. It was a subtle change at first, but eventually, became all too frequent.

Her father is largely responsible for this drastic change in her demeanor, due to the fact that he had been persistently teaching her to disrespect me all along. He was furnishing her with all the material things a girl could possibly want. He basically bought her anything she desired in his attempt to win her over. He was in a perfect position to do so. He has always lived under his parent's roof, even to this day. He has been collecting some pretty hefty disability checks for most of his life, even though he is more than capable of working if he really chose to do so. Truthfully, though, how would he ever have found the time to actually work? After all, he was entirely too busy spending every minute of his life trying to ruin mine.

As for me, I have always had to work for a living in order to support me and my daughter. My parents have long been deceased. I have always had to take care of myself and my daughter all on my own. Therefore, I could never compete with his lavish lifestyle nor would I choose to. It was never my intent to raise a spoiled, rotten brat. I had higher expectations for her than that. However, her father's overindulgence was increasingly starting to affect her. She began to expect me to give in to her every demand and if her demands were not met, she would react by screaming and yelling directly in my ears, ordering me to give in to her. When that didn't work, much to my dismay, she would then become physically abusive. She would either push or shove me and then, threaten to hit me or punch me with her fists if her demands were not met. When her demands were not satisfied, she didn't hesitate to carry out her threats. Occasionally, it would develop into violent rages where she would damage or destroy parts of my home. Any time she didn't get her way, she would threaten to call her father and tell him to pick her up because I was being mean to her.

One of the first serious confrontations that I've encountered between the two of us was involving a used bicycle that she wanted to buy. It was right after school had closed for summer break. My daughter saw a used bike at a local garage sale and decided she had to have it. Her dad had taken her bike with him when he moved out that past January. I was working the night shift and I had worked the night before. I laid down that morning to take a nap. I was abruptly woken up around 10:00 a.m. to the echoes of her yelling and screaming at me to get out of bed. She demanded that I get up immediately to take her to the place where this bicycle was so I could buy it for her. I told her that I had to work that night and I needed a little more sleep. I explained to her, if I was able to sleep until 3:00, then I would be better rested and I could look at the bike then. She insisted that I get up at that moment and she started throwing things at me in the bed to force me to get up right then. I hadn't had much sleep and she was getting on my last nerve. I finally did get up. I promised her if she could be patient, I would buy her a new bike when I received my next paycheck. However, that was not satisfactory with her. She wanted this particular bike because she could have it today for only $25.00. I explained that I didn't even have the $25.00 that was needed right then for the bike but she kept tormenting me with her temper outbursts and demanded I get her this bike that day and right then. She ended up throwing her book bag, full of hard-back books, directly at me, forcefully hitting me in my head. I have had only a couple hours of sleep at this point and was getting sick and tired of her unreasonable requests and abusive behaviors, so I picked up the book bag and lightly threw it back at her, but not nearly as hard as she threw it at me. I said, "Now, how did you like that? Well, I didn't like it when you threw it at my head either!" She then started screaming and crying and threatened to call her dad to come get her. I told her she would be grounded for her behavior that day and calling her dad to bail her out would only result in a stiffer punishment. She called him anyway. He came over, ranting and raving about how I had abused her and he was going to take her away from me because I was an abusive mother. I said she was not leaving with him. He kept arguing with me so I called the police. Fortunately, after I explained the situation to the police officer, who happened to be the police chief, himself, my daughter's father was advised to leave. My daughter was told that she had to stay with me because I was the custodial parent and my daughter had clearly done wrong. He went on to say that if she were his daughter; he would take her over his knee and give her a good spanking for her shameful behavior that day. Her dad left, reluctantly, and my daughter remained with me. She was not happy and neither was her father.

Unpleasant incidences, such as these, were becoming more and more common. The older she got, the more defiant she became. Every day was a constant battle. She argued with me morning 'til night, every chance she could. She didn't think she should have to mind me at all. At times, she would yell and scream at me so loudly, I wouldn't be surprised if the neighbors could hear it from miles away. Occasionally, she would hit or push me in her fits of anger. It was a very difficult time, to say the least. There were many times when

I felt feelings of hopelessness and despair because it seemed I was fighting this battle alone. Any time I would punish or ground her from privileges for a bad behavior, she would end up calling her father on her cell phone and he would come right over to bail her out. He would then use that opportunity to convince my daughter what a mean and terrible mother I was for punishing her in the first place.

She was becoming more and more unreasonable every day with her ridiculous demands. If there was something she suddenly desired or thought she just had to have, she expected me to give in to her at any given moment to accommodate her. When her demands were not met, she would become extremely angry and retaliate.

She thought she could leave my house and go anywhere she wanted at any time she wished. She believed there was no need to tell me where she was going or when she'd be back. Often times, she would ride her bike to her friend's house and come home after dark, knowing that was against the rules. When she had privileges taken away for breaking the rules and not minding me, she would become absolutely livid. At times she became enraged for no apparent reason at all. If I asked her what was making her so angry, she couldn't even tell me. I honestly don't believe she understood why. She simply found any excuse she could think of to pick a fight with me. Of course, she kept her dad well informed of any discipline that was ever given to her for unacceptable behavior because that's what he instructed her to do. He would then sympathize with her and tell her how terrible I was for punishing her at all. This was one of the many strategies he would use in his crazy attempt to brainwash her into believing I was an unfit mother.

On numerous occasions; she became so unruly that it became necessary to call law enforcement to my home. They provided very little relief. Some police officers dealt with my daughter's uncontrollable temper outbursts more appropriately than others but the majority of them were useless. I was quite often scolded for not being able to control my daughter's bad behavior on my own. I can recall one particular officer blatantly telling me, "You are the parent and you need to learn how to effectively handle your child!" Believe me, that is much easier said than done, especially, when you've got the other parent working against you, full force.

Even while this whole process of brainwashing was taking place, deep down, I truly believed I had a hold on the situation. In spite of all the agonizing pain my daughter was being subjected to and all the heartbreaking distress she was putting on me, we remained close for the most part. Apparently, that may have just been wishful thinking. Alas, my daughter began to play mind games between her father and I. She would express to me how she knew her dad was doing wrong and she didn't like how he lied and manipulated things to get his way. On the other hand, she began to make up lies herself, to tell her dad about my boyfriend and me. She would tell him anything that she thought he'd want to hear, just to keep him happy. When I eventually caught on to what she was doing, it hurt me terribly. That's when I started to finally realize, my daughter was growing up to be just like him. It was a devastating thought, but still, I couldn't give up on her. I love her too much for that. I continued to take her to counseling in the hopes that she and I would remain close. However, problems only got worst from that point on.

My biggest problem was getting her to go to school. Getting her to school in the mornings was becoming a major ordeal. There was just no reasoning with her. She hated school, though, she could never tell me why. I came to the conclusion that because of all the drama that her dad placed upon her combined with her learning disability, school probably required too much effort than my daughter was willing to give. I had a difficult time getting her to go on many occasions. I've had to file several unruly charges on her because she began physically lashing out at me. Numerous meetings were set up at school regarding her poor attendance. Her father never failed to try to make me look like the terrible parent in front of the school officials. He would always brag about how he never had any problems with our daughter, because he knew how to handle her better than I did. He would lay it on so thick; it made it exceptionally difficult to keep my composure.

Twice, my daughter was placed on a diversion program through the court system in an attempt to prevent her from missing the maximum amount of days that was permissible in one year. Even that didn't seem to help in the long-run. Her attendance remained poor. I was starting to feel like I was at the end of my rope.

Typically, when my daughter went through phases of oppositional behaviors, it would, generally, last for days, sometimes weeks at a time. It usually, started out with her not wanting to go to school. She would claim that her tummy hurt or she felt like throwing up. During one specific episode of not wanting to go to school, my daughter had just had a three day weekend, due to a holiday. When it came time to return on Tuesday, she said she was not feeling well and did not wish to go to school that day. She, clearly, was not truly sick so I tried my best to persuade her to go, but there was no getting through to her. Once she made up her mind to stay home, it was impossible to change it, no matter what. The more I tried to convince her to go, the more agitated she became. I was getting tired of arguing with her, once again, so on that particular morning, I decided to give up the fight for now and deal with her later, that evening. I had worked the night before and needed to get some sleep. However, she was told she must remain quiet and stay in bed the entire day. Of course, that didn't happen. My sleep got interrupted several times that day due to listening to her music too loud and noisily singing and jumping up and down on her bed while she was doing so. Because my daughter has A.D.H.D, she sometimes, had more energy than she could handle. I got up multiple times to tell her to keep it down, but she refused. She would lock me out of her bedroom so that I was not able to make her do as she was told. That night, I told her I would be taking her TV out of her room as punishment for her bad behaviors; arguing with me, turning her TV and radio too loud in her room, being too mouthy with me, and locking her bedroom door. I warned her way in advance, including that previous morning, that if she didn't go to school and kept on with her bad behaviors, her TV would be taken away. When I attempted to remove the TV from her room, my daughter became very irate. She continued to argue with me over the TV and then, she started to grab me by the arms, slapped my arms, and furiously tried to snatch the television out of my grasp. I went ahead and took it out of her room anyway. My daughter started slamming the doors. She slammed them with such force, that pictures were falling off the walls, one of them breaking. She tried to knock the kitchen chairs over and kicked the refrigerator so hard, it left a dent. Next, she began throwing lamps and anything else she could get a hold of. She pretty much followed me around the house the rest of the evening, badgering me to put her TV back in her room, but I did not.

On Wednesday morning, she, again, refused to go to school. I woke her up at 7:00. She said she was not going. I told her she had until 7:30, then, if she still was not ready, I would have to call the police. She proceeded to argue and yell at me the entire time. At 7:30, I took my phone and told her I'd give her one more chance; go to school and I would not have to make that call. She said she was not going, so I dialed the number. As I dialed, she tried to grab the phone from my hands. She started pushing me, punching me with her fists, and grabbing me by my arms. She continued this until the police arrived. She got a domestic charge and the police officer took her to school. She went to school the rest of the week. By the end of the week, I continued to have more problems with her.

On Friday evening, she went to another room of the house to watch TV, due to the fact that her TV had been taken away. She kept turning the volume up, just to annoy me. I told her if she didn't keep the TV at a reasonable volume, I would take that TV too. She got angry, threw the remote, and busted it to pieces. I sent her to her room with no TV. On Saturday morning, I was sleeping upstairs; I had worked the night before. At 1:30 in the afternoon, I woke up to hearing my daughter yelling and screaming at something she was watching on the television downstairs. She was in my living room, watching a wrestling program on my big screen TV. (I'll elaborate more about wrestling later) The remote was in her hand. She was jumping up and down and getting rambunctious on my furniture. I asked her why she was watching TV in the living room, when she was well aware that she wasn't allowed. I also asked her why she was making so much noise, when she knew I was still sleeping. She got very hateful with me. She said, if she didn't have a remote for the other TV, then she was going to watch it in the living room. I told her it wasn't going to work that way. I took the remote out of her hands and told her she would not be permitted to watch TV in the living room nor touch the remote for that TV after what she did to the other remote. I told her to get off the sofa, she would have to watch the other TV, even though it didn't have a remote, thanks to her busting it up. She got off the sofa, but before going to the other room; she punched my arm with her fist. She said, "That's what you get for taking my TV away from me." I grabbed her by the shoulders as she started to walk away. I told her she should be ashamed of herself for behaving the way she does, and if she continued to act in this manner, she will never get her TV back in her room and if she persisted to disrespect me and my household, there would be other consequences to pay. I told her that her behavior was totally unacceptable and it would not be tolerated.

The following Monday, she had an appointment with her psychologist at 4:00. Right after the appointment, my boyfriend and I wanted to take a walk across the road, on the trail by the river. It was a warm night and we tried to get my daughter to take a walk with us. She did not wish to go, so I told her she could stay in the vehicle, while my boyfriend and I took a 10 minute walk. Then, we would all go out to eat. She threw a temper tantrum over it. She followed us down the trail, yelling and screaming at us that she wanted to leave right now. My boyfriend told her to yell and scream all she wants; we were still going to take a short walk. That's when she ran up behind him and punched him as hard as she could in his back. My boyfriend turned around and firmly, took hold of her shoulders, and asked her to return to the van. We were going to continue our walk, in spite of her outburst. She kept on following us and harassing us the entire time. After our 10 minute walk, we all returned to the van. She immediately wanted to text her dad to tell him how my boyfriend had grabbed her and tried to hurt her, which obviously, was not true. I told her if she did that, I would take her phone away from her. She said I couldn't do that because that was her dad's phone. I told her I didn't care. As long as she was with me and misusing the phone in my presence, I had every right to take it from her. She continued arguing with me about it, but she finally decided not to text him. We went home, and what could have been an enjoyable evening for all of us, was ruined, but my daughter wouldn't have had it any other way.

My daughter's temper tantrums were becoming all too frequent. It got to the point where I couldn't feel comfortable going any place with her because she would somehow embarrass me with her inappropriate behavior and spoiled rotten attitude. I dreaded, just going to Wal-Mart with her to do grocery shopping. She would, in some way or another, create a nasty scene every time.

Following Christmas break, 2010, we went to Wal-Mart to exchange a gift. Right away, upon entering the store, she had found a pair of ear-rings she thought she had to have. She had been extremely disrespectful and mouthy to me during the whole drive there. I told her if she hadn't yelled and mouthed off so much, I may have bought them for her, but now I'm not. She threw a temper tantrum, like a 2 year old, and was getting quite loud in her angry fits of rage. She began yelling and screaming that I was such an awful mother because I never buy her anything. She then proceeded to push and shove, as well as, slap and punch me in her mad attempt to get me to give in to her. My boyfriend went ahead and gave her the money for the ear-rings, hoping to avoid a bigger scene than it already was. However, his hopes soon faded. She took the money and butted right in front of a long line of customers so that she didn't have to wait her turn. It was so humiliating that I apologized for her behavior and promptly exited the store. It was a long time before I mustered up enough courage to return. Unfortunately, many more horrific scenes such as this one were yet to come.

Ever since my daughter was a young girl, she had a habit of choosing some particular topic that would fascinate her and she would make it a main focus in her life. She would, then, create somewhat of a fantasy world for herself to escape to when things in the real world got too tough for her. This had always been a great concern of mine, but I was told by her mental health counselors, not to worry too much about it. They said that sort of behavior was not uncommon for children with learning disabilities. These types of children, sometimes, feel like they don't always fit in with other children who do not have learning disabilities, therefore, they sometimes create a fantasy world that they can escape to, once in a while. One of her first passions in life was country music. She knew everything there was to know about every country music star in Nashville. She listened to all their music and pretended to be a country music star, herself. Eventually, her interest in country music faded and she became captivated with teen music. Mylee Cyrus and the Jonas Brothers were among her favorites. It all seemed innocent, enough. But, then, one day, her father, introduced her to the world of wrestling mania. He exposed her to it with every visit. He bought her numerous DVD'S and wrestling magazines, most of them very inappropriate for her. She became fixated with a wrestler named Jeff Hardy.

Wrestling was having a very bad influence on my daughter. The more I stressed this to her father, the more he pushed it on her. Even school officials couldn't understand my concerns about her passion for wrestling. But, wrestling was taking over my daughter's life. It's all she ever talked about and she based everything she did in her life on wrestling and the characters on their shows. She even fantasized that she was Mrs. Jeff Hardy. She seemed to be living in the world of wrestling. She became so obsessed with wrestling that it was all she ever talked about from morning 'til night. It was very disturbing to me.

It was right about this time; I started noticing her sudden desire to alter her wardrobe attire. She decided that most everything she wore had to be black, right down to her lips and nail polish. It was somewhat unsettling. It was not only a drastic change for her but it was an eerie-looking one as well. I didn't want her to get a bad image so I tried to discourage it the best I could, but it was very difficult. She also started to wear weird looking jewelry, some of which was clearly repulsive.

That summer, my boyfriend and I took my daughter to the county fair. I was desperately hoping we could all have a good time enjoying the day together, but my daughter decided to totally spoil it. There was some jewelry at one of the booths in the coliseum that caught her eye. It was extremely offensive looking so I explained to her that I would be more than happy to buy her something else, other than that. She started yelling and arguing with me and she became so angry that she threw the cup of soda pop in her hands right in my face, spilling it all over me. I was so mortified that naturally, we left immediately to go back home. Her indifferent attitude towards me was making it nearly impossible to enjoy spending any time with her at all.

In February of 2010, yet, another major dilemma had taken place in my life, involving my daughter. We were in the middle of a Level 3 snow storm. School had been cancelled for a few days so my daughter was bound and determined to spend the extra time at her dad's house. I found out, later, it was because he let her watch wrestling, non-stop, any time she wanted to, which was pretty much constant. He also had all the wrestling magazines and DVD's that were ever published or produced for her viewing pleasure. I totally disagreed with the amount of wrestling she was being exposed to because I could see it having a very bad effect on my daughter. She was becoming much more aggressive and belligerent and downright violent. The more I protested, the more he let her watch it and the more she watched it, the more it became a number one priority in her life. Knowing that I wouldn't allow her to watch wrestling night and day, like she could when she was with her dad, she decided to stay with him during the snow days. It was a welcome break for me, but after one night with him, I found out that her dad had signed her out from school one afternoon without my knowledge, prior to school being cancelled. One of the school officials had called me to ask me if I was aware of that, which I was not. It turned out, her dad had signed her out to go with him somewhere, even though her attendance was poor and she couldn't afford any more unnecessary absences. When I called her to ask her why her dad had signed her out, she said it was for a doctor's appointment that her dad had made for her. I thought her story sounded fishy because I have always been the one to take her to the doctor when needed. So, I called the doctor's office to verify what she had told me. They said that my daughter did not have an appointment and was never seen. I called my daughter back and questioned her about her so-called doctor appointment. She proceeded to tell me that, yes; she had been seen by the doctor. I told her I had called the doctor's office and checked and so I knew she was not telling the truth. She hesitated, but, finally, had no choice but to admit she had lied. However, neither she nor her dad would tell me where they went. I informed her that I would be picking her up at Dad's house that evening, in spite of the bad weather because I wasn't going to tolerate her lying to me. She was furious and said that she wasn't going to come with me. I told her if she didn't cooperate, I would have to involve the police. She did, come home with me, but not very willingly. She was fuming mad. Ever since this whole wrestling obsession began, my daughter started dressing very inappropriately. She would wear clothes that were, somewhat, provocative. Her father bought her anything she desired. She also started wearing knee high leather boots with very high heels. She had leather bracelets and big hooped ear-rings and she would, basically, end up looking like a slut. We were constantly arguing about her attire, but it was getting increasingly difficult trying to get her to wear anything that she didn't wish to wear. Now, getting back to the dilemma. Of course, she was wearing her boots with the big heels that day I brought her back from her dad's house. I warned her not to go up or down the stair steps, wearing those boots because it was too dangerous, but naturally, she didn't listen. She continuously badgered me to take her back to Dad's house because she didn't want to miss her wrestling shows, but I stuck to my guns and refused to give in. I went upstairs to my bedroom to escape her torment, but she followed me up there, in her boots. She kicked the wall in the stair-well as she was going up; then, she hit my closet door with her fist, creating a dent. At this point, I had just about had enough. I threatened to call the police if she didn't leave my room and go back downstairs. She shouted, "I hate you, Mom!", and then, in her mad attempt to head down the stairs, she tripped on one of her heels and fell down the steps with such force, that when she hit the corner of the staircase, it split the center of her nose wide open. It required a trip to the emergency room, where she received numerous stitches in her nose. To top it off, she tried to tell the nurses that I had pushed her. Thank God, they saw through her lies.

I don't know how I ever lasted 'til the end of the school year, without losing my sanity. My daughter's evil attitude and wicked behaviors were turning my life into a dreadful nightmare. I felt like I was constantly under attack. Every day brought a new challenge and I never knew what to expect from one day to the next. However, sometime during the very last month of school, my daughter's class participated in a field trip at the Career Technical Center. This was a joint vocational school which they were entitled to enroll in their junior and senior year if they so chose. My daughter was thrilled with the prospect of switching schools. She was quite impressed with the school itself and what it had to offer. Because of her disability, her career choices were limited, but she was able to enter into the field of hospitality. It wasn't the career field she would have, personally chosen for herself, but it was acceptable to her and seemed to be a good fit. So, as that school year came to a close, my daughter appeared to be very happy with herself and that made me very happy.

Her summer vacation had its ups and downs. She enjoyed her time off and so did I. It was a great relief to get a break from having to continuously fight with her, trying to get her to go to school. She showed so much enthusiasm towards her new school that I couldn't help but feel a small bit of optimism, in the hopes that things might turn around for my daughter, after all. However, my daughter's obsession with wrestling was rapidly growing and getting out of control. She, increasingly, became compelled to be just like the uninhibited women on the wrestling programs. She continued to dress and act like them more and more every day. They were extremely promiscuous and vulgar and my daughter was mesmerized by them. There was one wrestling girl, in particular, that my daughter was quite enticed with. She had bright red hair and multiple ill-mannered tattoos. My daughter began to express her wishes to get a tattoo and dye her hair bright red. I said, "Absolutely not!" She desired it so badly that she begged me, tirelessly, to allow her to dye her hair bright red. She nagged me for days, insisting that I let her do it, but I refused to give in to her. That week-end, right before school was to begin, her grandma had gone ahead and without my permission, dyed my daughter's hair bright red during her visitation with her dad. When she returned home, I was shocked and appalled when I saw her with bright red hair. She looked like a clown, but my daughter was quite proud of herself. School was about to begin on the following Monday and I knew that her bright red hair would be unacceptable. Sure enough, when she arrived at school on the first day, she was told that she must change her hair color back to a normal shade. My daughter protested, but had no choice. She was very upset with her teacher for making her change her hair back to the original color. She didn't like her teacher from that point on. She got in constant trouble by refusing to follow school rules, but in spite of it all, her attendance remained satisfactory. However, right after Christmas break had ended, she started showing dis-interest, once again. I began having the same problems as before, only much worse. It became necessary to place her back in the court system on the diversion program, in an attempt to get her to go to school. I had to call police officers to the house from time to time because her attendance was becoming too infrequent. The more I pressured her to go to school, the more frustrated and agitated she would become. Sometimes, she would become violent, by destroying parts of my house or by pounding her fists on me. She even attempted pulling me down the stairs while trying to grab the phone from my hand. Eventually, she got caught exhibiting pornographic material on her school computer. She received in-school suspension for that and had her computer taken away for two weeks. Apparently, while she was serving the in-school suspension, she was busy writing a very sexually explicit letter, elaborating about her sexual encounters with Jeff Hardy and other wrestling figures. The letter was extensive and extraordinarily graphic. She went into great detail, about unspeakable sexual acts as well as sexual torture involving all the wrestling characters. I was utterly and completely horrified, and that's putting it mildly. Not surprisingly, this resulted in an immediate expulsion. This meant that she would have to return to her previous school and she was not happy with that, what-so-ever. Things spiraled downward from that point on. My daughter was angry and became even more verbally and physically abusive towards my boyfriend and I after that.

My daughter's inappropriate and totally offensive behaviors were, without a doubt, a direct result of what she learned from her father during her visits with him. The excessive amount of wrestling that she was exposed to at her dad's house, obviously, had an evil effect on her, as I have predicted. Of course, he denied it and insisted that I was to blame because I was the custodial parent. How typical!

School officials bent over backwards to get my daughter back on track at her former school. They fit her into the schedule and rearranged her classes as quickly and beneficially as possible. This was a difficult task, being so close to the end of the school year, but they went out of their way to try to help her. At the time, she promised to go to school for the rest of the school year. However, since then, I have had continuous problems with her. I proceeded to take privileges away from her as a consequence for not going to school and for disrespecting me. First, I took access to the computer away from her. For weeks, she kept hounding me to give it back to her. She tore my house up, looking for it. She found it, once, and fought with me, trying to get it back. I told her, all she had to do was go to school and stop arguing with me all the time. If she could do that, she could get the computer back, but I would still have to monitor her while using it. She had a fit and began to push, shove, poke, and kick me. I refused to give in, but she made my life a living hell. When I continued having issues with getting her to go to school and disrespecting me, I took TV access away from her, especially programs regarding the wrestling that she was so obsessed with. When I wouldn't give her the password to watch a wrestling program that was due to come on at 9:00 that evening on Thursday, April 28th, she became furious. I had prewarned her that same morning, that if she didn't go to school that day, she would not be permitted to watch her wrestling program that night. She said she didn't care and stayed home anyway. So, that evening, starting at approximately 3:00, she began taunting and tormenting me to give her the password for her wrestling shows that came on at 9:00. I kept telling her no and I reminded her that she had been warned that this would be her consequence and she said she didn't care. I would not give her the password. So every 10 or 15 minutes from 3:00 to 9:00, she would come out of her room to pressure me into giving in to her. She would poke at me and scream in my ear that I'd better give her the password; otherwise, she threatened to hit me. When I would not give her the password, she proceeded to hit me. She tried to hit me in the chest, face, and stomach. So, I put my arms out in front of me to protect myself, somewhat. I threatened to call the police if she continued, but I hesitated, hoping she would get tired of fighting with me, after a while, when I wouldn't give in to her. She persisted with this behavior all evening. She would begin by poking me in the shoulder, then, she would push me, then, hit me with her fists. She would, periodically, kick me. My boyfriend came home around 8:00. He saw what she was doing to me and pulled her off of me. She, then, started fighting with him. He held her against the wall, trying to get her to calm down. When she finally did, she headed towards her bedroom, but as she passed me, she shoved me so vigorously, it nearly knocked me down. She then proceeded to forcefully hit me in my arm. My boyfriend grabbed her by the shoulders and held her down on the futon. He told her that he wasn't going to let her hit me while he was there. She finally went back to her bedroom, but soon after came out and started fighting with us again. She kept insisting that I give her the password.

She, repeatedly, shoved the remote in my hand. I'd put the remote down and told her she wasn't getting the password. She kept picking it up and shoving it in my hand. This continued for a while, until she finally got frustrated and forcefully threw the remote on the floor. I picked it up and told her she wasn't getting it back. Then, she started pushing me around, trying to get it back. This went on for a while. My boyfriend told her, repeatedly, throughout the rest of the evening, how she should be ashamed of herself for treating her mother so abusively and with such a lack of respect. She didn't want to hear it, so, as my boyfriend sat on the couch, my daughter came up from behind him, un-expectantly, and forcefully hit him in the back of his head. She retorted, "You are not my dad and I don't have to listen to you!" Finally, I couldn't take it anymore. As a last ditch effort, I made a deal with her. I told her I would set the password this one time, but this behavior would have to stop immediately. I explained to her that she absolutely could not miss any more school for the remainder of the year. If she broke her end of the bargain, I would take the TV out of her room, permanently. She said she was sorry and promised she would change her behavior. However, Friday morning, April 29th, I woke her up for school and she said she had a back-ache and couldn't go. I explained, again, what her consequences would be and kept trying to convince her to do the right thing. She got agitated and began screaming at me to let her alone. When I continued talking to her, she started coming after me, hitting and pushing. I finally concluded that I had no other choice but to call the police. As I turned around to dial the number, she came up from behind me and punched me in the middle of my back, so robustly, that it nearly knocked the air right out of me. When the police arrived, after some serious discussion, we decided to send her to detention for a day or two. It broke my heart to send her there, but I was at my wit's end and felt I had no other option. Nothing else, I've tried seemed to work. This was a last resort. She begged and pleaded with me not to make her go, but after all she had put me through, as heart-breaking as it was, I knew I couldn't turn back now. So they took her away.

I had only planned on her staying in detention for one or two days, but once you involve the courts, your life and general well-being is entirely in their hands. The juvenile judge had ordered her to stay a full seven days. Her father had visited her while being detained and quickly moved in with his brainwashing tactics. It wasn't too difficult to figure out what damaging thoughts he had programmed into her head. I was a terrible mother for allowing her to be placed in detention and I couldn't possibly love her as much as he does. She would be so much better off if she would come live with him because he would never do such a despicable thing like that to her. I was an abusive mother and she didn't need me in her life. I can only imagine all the hateful things that were drilled into her head at that time. He never missed an opportunity to drag me down in the mud in his attempt to make me look like the bad parent. Upon being released, a court hearing was held and naturally, my daughter requested to live with her father. I explained to the judge that I didn't feel it was in my daughter's best interest to live with him and I wanted to be able to mend my relationship with my daughter as soon as possible. I wanted to make her better understand why she got sent to detention. It wasn't because I wanted it that way, which is what her father has convinced her of, I'm sure. In spite of my plea, the judge allowed her to go with her dad, since that was her wish to do so and she was so close to turning 18. He gave temporary custody to her father. His father's parents were also there, supporting their son as they always have in all of his wrong-doing. The relationship between my daughter's father and his mother was often strained; however, he and his father remained very close. They are both well aware of how disturbed he is, but he is their son and they have chosen to stand by him. Their interference was uncalled for and has contributed to the alienation between my daughter and me. They told the judge that they would step in and help their son in any way they could. Their son was living under their roof and always had, so my daughter would be staying with them as well. They did not help the situation. They only helped it get from bad to worse.

PARENTAL ALIENATION IS ABUSE

My daughter was also ordered by the court to write me a letter of apology and continue to attend family counseling with her father and me. As for the written apology, it wasn't worth the paper it was written on, it meant nothing. It was totally insincere and was only done because of the order.

As for the counseling, it never happened, which was not surprising. Within a week after the hearing, she returned to my house to retrieve her belongings. When I opened the door to let her in, she barged right past me, forcefully nudging me in my side. She had such an evil look of contempt in her eyes and spoke with me in such a hateful tone, stating, "I've come to get my stuff and you can't stop me!" After all that had happened, I wasn't about to let her continue to dis-respect me in my home any longer. So I decided to call a police officer over for our protection. What a huge mistake! This particular so-called officer handled the whole situation very inappropriately. I don't know what his problem was that evening. Maybe he was tired of having to come to my house so frequently during the past year when my daughter became unruly. Or perhaps he had a tough childhood, himself. It's a known fact that he came from a broken home, so maybe he has been affected by it. Whatever his problem, he definitely mishandled everything. My daughter was treated as if she was the victim and my boyfriend and I were treated like common criminals. My daughter was attempting to take things from her room that were not personally hers and I was not about to reward her for her bad behavior by letting her have them. She thought she could take the TV and DVD player she had been using, but I wouldn't let her. It wasn't hers. Then, she tried to take a bucket which was filled with various bottles of nail polish. This, also, was not hers. We shared this nail polish, but she was adamant about taking it. When she picked up the bucket, I told her I did not want her to have it because I use it also. I knew she had more at her dad's house, but she insisted on taking it anyway. The officer was going to allow her to take it, but I told him that it was not specifically hers to take and I did not wish for her to have it. My boyfriend, who was standing nearby, reached over to take the bucket from her hands, per my request. My daughter quickly snatched it back from him and frantically held on to it. I was standing in the doorway, and next thing we knew, the officer had pulled out his Taser gun, held my boyfriend against the wall, and threatened to use it on him. He accused him of forcefully grabbing my daughter by her wrist, which couldn't be further from the truth. He was only trying to take back what was not hers to take and she was the forceful one. When I rushed to his side in his defense, the officer threatened to use the Taser on me also. I told him that he could go ahead and use the Taser if he so wished, but my daughter was not taking the nail polish. He then, ordered her to gather what she could within 15 minutes; at which time she would have to leave. Upon leaving,

I told my daughter that I loved her more than anything in the world, but I wasn't going to put up with her disrespect any longer. I also told her that she need not return until she was truly sorry for her actions and was willing to change. Needless to say, the effects of that evening have probably scarred me and my boyfriend for life, as well as my daughter. The next day, I called the county sheriff's office to file a complaint against this officer, but the police chief was on vacation that week. I was told to call back when he returned, but I never did. I couldn't handle any more trauma and after thinking about it, I honestly didn't know if it would have done any good. The damage had already been done.

Subsequently, I have not had any contact with my daughter since that day. Looking back, it's hard to fathom how things could have gotten so out of hand. I thought that some temporary time apart, would make her realize the value of a loving mother who only wanted the very best for her daughter by trying to teach her to be a decent, caring, and responsible human being. Unfortunately, that did not happen, as of yet. I love my daughter with all my heart, but my heart has been broken. If I give in and contact her, things will remain as they were. I don't even know for certain if she realizes the extent of the pain and suffering she and her father have caused or if she will ever have remorse for what she has done. Maybe she thinks I am the one that hurt her. Children with learning disabilities don't always think rationally, especially with another irrational person, above all, a parent, telling them how to feel. All I know is this. No child or parent should ever have to go through a deceitful, destructible, and hurtful act such as parent alienation. It's a sad situation, but I now have no other choice but to accept it and move on. Hopefully, as time goes by, my daughter will understand how things really are. I was never the mean, abusive mother that her father had made me out to be. I was just a caring mother whose number one concern was my daughter's happiness and well-being. I sincerely believe that someday, I will be reunited with my daughter, but until then, I'm taking it one day at a time.

Conclusion

Six years ago, when my daughter's original custody papers were written and signed in the court of law, it was clearly stated in black and white that mutual respect was expected to be given between parents during situations regarding the children. Sadly, the courts fail to enforce this.

Growing up in today's society is difficult enough for a child to endure. Teaching a child such extreme hatred and disrespect should never be acceptable. Hatred hurts and nothing good ever comes of it. Sometimes it even kills.

No child should be forced to choose one parent over the other or be taught to disrespect the other parent. No loving, caring, honorable parent would ever even consider putting their child in that torturous situation. Any parent who willingly commits this extremely hateful and destructive act does not have their child's best interest at heart. They are

PARENTAL ALIENATION IS ABUSE

only putting their own selfish needs in front of their child's.

It is unfortunate, as in my case that the courts and mental health officials failed to foresee or prevent the destructive outcome that parental alienation can and has resulted in. A more favorable outcome might have happened if court proceedings had been handled with more care and efficiency.

For instance, court orders should be strictly enforced and carried out, no exceptions. If one parent does not adhere to them, (family counseling or visitation times and schedules for example), then that parent needs to be accountable and promptly charged with contempt of court; therefore, being punished accordingly, and not just given a slap on the hand. If counseling is recommended and ordered by the courts, mental health officials should be required to report pertinent information in a timely manner. Then, if any inappropriate talk or behavior is exhibited and determined to be detrimental to the child's well-being, necessary steps should be promptly taken. For example, the requirement to take parenting classes along with additional counseling. Supervised visits should be arranged involving the children in extreme circumstances, such as mine, until the problem is remedied. A strong message needs to be given to alienating parents and that is, parent alienation is harmful and causes extreme, life-long mental distress to the child as well as the alienated parent and it will not be tolerated. Parent alienation is abuse and needs to be acknowledged as such.

Schools, also, should get more involved by implementing prevention intervention programs for our students concerning divorce and custody. Studies show that 25% or more children of divorce will suffer emotional trauma as a result of their parent's actions which ultimately contributes to other serious behavior problems that may include, but are not limited to: aggression, depression, attention deficit disorder, poor academic performance, bullying, and oppositional defiance disorder.

Studies also show that parents are more apt to attend counseling sessions in the schools before agreeing to outside services. This means that, school personnel, can help the students if they step up to the plate and offer services to the family unit.

In my own personal case, I can only hope that; through therapy, time, and patience, the loving bond that my daughter and I once shared can be restored one day. An immense amount of damage has taken place, so I have to accept the fact that the close-knit relationship we had in the beginning most likely will never be the same. However, I have gained some valuable insight during my past experiences while trying to cope with parental alienation. It is very important to keep

PARENTAL ALIENATION IS ABUSE

your emotions under control, no matter how difficult that may be. It is vital that you remain logical, even-tempered and never retaliate. A person who reacts in anger is proving the alienator's point that he or she is unstable. Also, above all, continue trying to get the courts to understand the seriousness of the issues of parental alienation to the point that they may see the need to take action. If enough parents step forward and speak up and demand to be heard, only then, we might begin to make a difference. Only then, they might finally realize how unjust this horrible abuse really is.

Parental Alienation (htt)

Parental Alienation varies in the degree of severity, as seen in the behaviors and attitudes of both the parents and the children. The severity can be of such little consequence as a parent occasionally calling the other parent a derogatory name; or it could be as overwhelming as the parent's campaign of consciously destroying the children's relationship with the other parent. Most children are able to brush off a parent's offhand comment about the other parent that is made in frustration. On the other hand, children may not be able to resist a parent's persistent campaign of hatred and alienation.

Preventing or stopping alienation must begin with learning how to recognize the three types of alienators because the symptoms and strategies for combating each are different. Naïve alienators are parents who are passive about the children's relationship with the other parent but will occasionally do or say some-

PARENTAL ALIENATION IS ABUSE

thing to alienate. All parents will occasionally be naïve alienators. Active alienators know better than to alienate, but their intense hurt or anger causes them to impulsively lose control over their behavior or what they say. Later, they may feel very guilty about how they behaved. Obsessed alienators have a fervent cause, to destroy the targeted parent. Frequently, a parent can be a blend between two types of alienators, usually a combination between the naïve and active alienator. Rarely does the obsessed alienator have enough self-control or insight to blend with the other types.

Understanding the Three Different Types of Alienation

The Naïve Alienator

"Tell your father that he has more money than I do, so let him buy your soccer shoes."

Most divorced parents have moments when they are Naïve alienators. These parents mean well and recognize the importance of the children having a healthy relationship with the other parent. They rarely have to return to court because of problems with visits or other issues relating to the children. They encourage the relationship between the children and the other parent and their family. Communication between both parents is usually good, though they will have their disagreements, much like they did before the divorce. For the most part, they can work out their differences without bringing the children into it.

Children, whether or not their parents are divorced, know there are times when their parents will argue or disagree about something. They don't like seeing their parents argue and may feel hurt or frightened by what they hear. Somehow, the children manage to cope, either by talking out their feelings to a receptive parent, ignoring the argument or trusting that the skirmish will pass and all will heal. What they see and hear between their parents does not typically damage the children of the Naïve alienator. They trust their parent's love and protection. The child and the parent have distinct personalities, beliefs, and feelings. Neither is threatened by how the other feels toward the targeted parent.

The characteristics of Naive alienators are:

- Their ability to separate in their minds the children's needs from their own. They recognize the importance for the children to spend time with the other parent so they can build a mutually loving relationship. They avoid making the other parent a target for their hurt and loss.

- Their ability to feel secure with the children's

relationship with their grandparents and their mother or father.

- Their respect for court orders and authority.

- Their ability to let their anger and hurt heal and not interfere with the children's relationship with their mother or father.

- Their ability to be flexible and willing to work with the other parent.

- Their ability to feel guilty when they acted in a way to hurt the children's relationship with their mother or father.

- Their ability to allow the other parent to share in their children's activities.

- Their ability to share medical and school records.

Naïve alienators usually don't need therapy but will benefit from learning about parental alienation because of the insight they will gain about how to keep alienation from escalating into something more severe and damaging for all. These parents know they make mistakes but care enough about their children to make things right. They focus on what is good for the children without regret, blame, or martyrdom.

The Active Alienator:

"I don't want you to tell your father that I earned this extra money. The miser will take it from his child support check that will keep us from going to Disneyworld. You remember he's done this before when we wanted to go to Grandma's for Christmas."

Most parents returning to court over problems with visitation are active alienators. These parents mean well and believe that the children should have a healthy relationship with the other parent. The problem they have is with controlling their frustration, bitterness, or hurt. When something happens to trigger their painful feelings, active alienators lash out in a way to cause or reinforce alienation against the targeted parent. After regaining control, the parent will usually feel guilty or bad about what they did and back off from their alienating tactics. Vacillating between impulsively alienating and then repairing the damage with the children is the trademark of the active alienator.

They mean well, but will lose control because the intensity of their feelings overwhelms them.

The characteristics of active alienators are:

- Lashing out at the other parent in front of the children. Their problem has more to do with loss of self-control when they are upset than with a sinister motivation.

- After calming down, active alienators realize that they were wrong. They usually try to repair any damage or hurt to the children. During the making up, such parents can be very comforting and supportive of the child's feelings.

- Like naive alienators, they are able to differentiate between their needs and those of the children by supporting the children's desire to have a relationship with the other parent.

- Like naive alienators, active alienators allow the children to have different feelings and beliefs from their own. During the flare ups of anger, however, the delineation between the child and parent's beliefs can become very blurry until the parent calms down and regains control. For the most part, older children have their own opinions about both parents based upon personal experience rather than what they are told by others. To keep peace, the older child usually learns to keep their opinions to themselves. Younger and more trusting children become more confused and vulnerable to their parents' manipulations.

PARENTAL ALIENATION IS ABUSE

They have the ability to respect the court's authority and, for the most part, comply with court orders. However, they can be very rigid and uncooperative with the other parent. This is usually a passive attempt to strike back at the other parent for some injustice. Active alienators are usually willing to accept professional help when they or the children have a problem that does not go away. They are sincerely concerned about their children's adjustment to the divorce. Harboring old feelings continues to be a struggle, but active alienators continue to hope for a speedy recovery from their pain.

The Obsessed Alienator

"I love my children. If the court can't protect them from their abusive father, I will. Even though he's never abused the children, I know it's a matter of time. The children are frightened of their father. If they don't want to see him, I'm not going to force them. They are old enough to make up their own minds."

The obsessed alienator is a parent, or sometimes a grandparent, with a cause: to align the children to his or her side and together, with the children, campaign to destroy their relationship with the targeted parent. For the campaign to work, the obsessed alienator enmeshes the children's personalities and beliefs into their own. This is a process that takes time but one that the children, especially the young, are completely helpless to see and combat. It usually begins well before the divorce is final. The obsessed parent is angry, bitter or feels betrayed by the other parent. The initial reasons for the bitterness may actually be justified. They could have been verbally and physical abused, raped, betrayed by an affair, or financially cheated. The problem occurs when the feelings won't heal but instead become more intense because of being forced to continue the relationship with a person they despise because of their common parenthood. Just having to see or talk to the other parent is a reminder of the past and triggers the hate. They are trapped with nowhere to go and heal.

The characteristics of obsessed alienators are:

- They are obsessed with destroying the children's relationship with the targeted parent.

- They having succeeded in enmeshing the children's personalities and beliefs about the other parent with their own.

- The children will parrot the obsessed alienator rather than express their own feelings from personal experience with the other parent.

- The targeted parent and often the children cannot tell you the reasons for their feelings.

PARENTAL ALIENATION IS ABUSE

Their beliefs sometimes becoming delusional and irrational. No one, especially the court, can convince obsessed alienators that they are wrong. Anyone who tries is the enemy.

- They will often seek support from family members, quasi-political groups or friends that will share in their beliefs that they are victimized by the other parent and the system. The battle becomes "us against them." The obsessed alienator's supporters are often seen at the court hearings even though they haven't been subpoenaed.

- They have an unquenchable anger because they believe that they have been victimized by the targeted parent and whatever they do to protect the children is justified.

- They have a desire for the court to punish the other parent with court orders that would interfere or block the targeted parent from seeing the children. This confirms in the obsessed alienator's mind that he or she was right all the time. The court's authority does not intimidate them.

- The obsessed alienator believes in a higher cause, protecting the children at all cost.

- The obsessed alienator will probably not want

UNDERSTANDING THE THREE DIFFERENT TYPES OF ALIENATION

to read what is on these pages because the content just makes them angrier.

There are no effective treatments for either the obsessed alienator or the children. The courts and mental health professionals are helpless. The only hope for these children is early identification of the symptoms and prevention. After the alienation is entrenched and the children become "true believers" in the parent's cause, the children are lost to the other parent for years to come. We realize this is a sad statement, but we have yet to find an effective intervention, by anyone, including the courts that can rehabilitate the alienating parent and child.

As a divorced parent, you worry when the other parent makes derogatory remarks and tries to give your child a negative image of you. But when do mere derogatory remarks turn into a harmful psychological phenomenon that psychologists have labeled the "parental alienation syndrome"?

Parental alienation syndrome occurs when one parent's efforts to consciously or unconsciously brainwash a child combine with the child's own bad-mouthing of the other parent. In severe cases, the child won't want to see or talk to the alienated parent.

Once the alienation reaches such a point, it's difficult to reverse, and permanent damage is done to the child and to the relationship between the child and the alienated parent.

Warning Signs of Parental Alienation

How can you tell if your ex is attempting to alienate your child? Here are some warning symptoms psychologists have observed in children suffering from parental alienation syndrome, according to Dr. Douglas Darnall, Ph.D:

- Giving a child a choice as to whether or not to visit with the other parent.

- Telling the child details about the marital relationship or reasons for the divorce.

- Refusing to acknowledge that the child has property and may want to transport possessions between residences.

- Resisting or refusing to cooperate by not allowing the other parent access to school or medical records and schedules of extracurricular activities.

- One parent blaming the other parent for financial problems, breaking up the family, changes in lifestyle, or having a girlfriend or boyfriend.

UNDERSTANDING THE THREE DIFFERENT TYPES OF ALIENATION

- Refusing to be flexible with the visitation schedule in order to respond to the child's needs, or scheduling the child in so many activities that the other parent is never given the time to visit.

- Assuming that if a parent has been physically abusive with the other parent, it follows that the parent will assault the child. This assumption is not always true.

- Asking the child to choose one parent over the other.

- The alienating parent encouraging any natural anger the child has toward the other parent.

- A parent or stepparent suggesting changing the child's name or having the stepparent adopt the child.

- When the child can't give reasons for being angry towards a parent or gives reasons that are vague and without any details.

- Using a child to spy or covertly gather information for the parent's own use.

- Arranging temptations that interfere with the other parent's visitation.

- Reacting with hurt or sadness to a child having a good time with the other parent.

- Asking the child about the other parent's personal life.

- Physically or psychologically rescuing a child when there's no threat to their safety.

- Making demands on the other parent that are contrary to court orders.

- Listening in on the child's phone conversation with the other parent.

What Causes Parental Alienation?

What causes a parent to want to damage the relationship of their own child with the other parent at their own child's expense? Intentions differ from one parent to the next, but psychologists have suggested the following as potential motivators:

- An alienating parent may have unresolved anger toward the other parent for perceived wrongs during the relationship and may be unable to separate those issues from parenting issues.

- An alienating parent may have unresolved issues from their childhood, particularly in how

UNDERSTANDING THE THREE DIFFERENT TYPES OF ALIENATION

they related to their own parents, which he or she projects onto the other parent (whether or not it's factually accurate).

- An alienating parent may have a personality disorder, such as narcissism or paranoia, which makes him or her unable to empathize with the child's feelings or see the way their behavior is harming the child. Such personality disorders may also make the alienating parent more likely to be jealous of the other parent's adjustment to the breakup and cause the alienating parent to have extreme rage toward the other parent.

- An alienating parent may be so insecure as to his or her own parenting skills that he or she projects those concerns onto the other parent, regardless of reality.

- An alienating parent may be so wrapped up in their child's life that he or she has no separate identity and sees the child's relationship with the other parent as a threat.

- Sometimes new spouses or grandparents push the alienating parent into inappropriate behavior for their own inappropriate reasons, and the alienating parent isn't strong enough to resist them.

◄ PARENTAL ALIENATION IS ABUSE

What causes a child to buy into the alienating parent's brainwashing? The child may:

- Feel the need to protect a parent who's depressed, panicky or needy

- Want to avoid the anger or rejection of a dominant parent, who's also often the custodial parent

- Want to hold onto the parent the child is most afraid of losing, such as a parent who is self-absorbed or not very involved with the child.

In choosing to go along with the viewpoint of the alienating parent, the child can avoid conflict and remove him or herself from the constant tug-of-war.

How Does Alienation Occur?

The alienating parent may use a number of techniques, including but not limited to:

- Encouraging the child to pretend the other parent doesn't exist. This can range from not allowing the child to mention the other parent's name to refusing to acknowledge that the child has fun with the other parent.

- Leading the child to believe it's his or her

choice as to whether or not to spend time with the other parent.

- Attacking the other parent's character or lifestyle, such as job, living arrangements, planned activities with the child, clothing and friends (particularly new romantic partners).

- Putting the child in the middle, by encouraging the child to spy on the other parent or take messages back and forth.

- Emphasizing the other parent's flaws, such as an occasional burst of temper or not being prepared for the child's activities. Normal parental lapses are blown out of proportion and the child is repeatedly reminded of them.

- Discussing court battles between the parents with the child and encouraging the child to take sides.

- Making the child think there's reason to be afraid of the other parent.

- Lying about how the other parent treats the child. If this is done frequently enough, the child may begin to believe even preposterous suggestions.

- Rewriting history, such as suggesting to the child that the other parent never cared for him or her, even as an infant. The child has no memory of prior events and so can't determine whether the alienating parent is telling the truth or not.

What Does An Alienated Child Look Like?

A child who's been successfully alienated:

- Will bad-mouth the other parent with foul language and inaccurate descriptions of the other parent.

- Offer only weak or frivolous reasons for his or her anger toward the targeted parent.

- Professes to have only hatred toward the targeted parent, and can't say anything positive about them.

- Insists that he or she is solely responsible for the attitude toward the other parent, and that the alienating parent had nothing to do with his or her attitude.

- Supports and feels protective toward the alienating parent.

- Doesn't show any empathy or guilt regarding hurting the targeted parent's feelings.

- Doesn't want anything to do with the targeted parent's friends and family.

- May not want to see or talk to the alienated parent.

What should you do if you fear the other parent is trying to alienate your child?

If you are a parent who is a victim of the parental alienation syndrome, it may have struck without warning and you're wracking your brain trying to figure out what happened. Many alienated parents find it difficult to control their anger and hurt over being treated so poorly by their child and ex-spouse.

Experts on alienation suggest the following as ways to cope with the problem:*

- Try to control your anger and stay calm and in control of your own behavior.

- Keep a log of events as they happen, describing in detail what happened and when.

- Always call or pick up your child at scheduled times, even when you know the child won't be available. This is likely to be painful, but you must be able to document to the court that you tried to see your child and were refused.

PARENTAL ALIENATION IS ABUSE

- During time spent with your child, focus on positive activities, and reminisce with the child about previous good times you had together.

- Never discuss the court case with your child.

- Try not to argue with or be defensive with your child. Focus on talking openly about what your child is actually seeing and feeling, as opposed to what the child has been told to be the truth.

- Work on improving your parenting skills by taking parenting courses, reading parenting books, etc., so that you can be the best possible parent to your child.

- If possible, get counseling for your child, preferably with a therapist trained to recognize and treat parental alienation syndrome. If it's not possible to get your child into counseling, go to counseling yourself to learn how to react to and counteract the problem.

- Don't do anything to violate any court orders or otherwise be an undesirable parent. Pay your child support on time and fulfill all your parenting obligations to the letter.

- Don't react to the alienating behavior by engaging in alienating behavior toward your ex. This just makes things worse and further harms the child.

- If you're not getting court-ordered time with your child, go back to court and ask that the parent violating the court order be held in contempt of court. The sooner the court knows about the violation of the court order, the more likely it is that the problem can be stopped before it becomes permanent and irreversible. If your custody order isn't specific as to exact times and dates you're to be with the child, ask the court to make the order very specific so that there can be no doubt what is required.

- Try not to blame your child. Your child didn't create the situation and desperately needs your love and affection.

Questions for Your Attorney

- Is it okay to say negative comments about the parent in front of my children?

- What if my children say negative comments about the other parent? Should I try to stop them?

- How can I stop the other parent from saying negative comments about me? (htt)

Parental Alienation Syndrome is Child Abuse

By Richard A. Gardner, M.D.

- It is important for examiners to appreciate that a parent who inculcates a PAS in a child is indeed perpetrating a form of emotional abuse in that such programming may not only produce lifelong alienation from a loving parent, but lifelong psychiatric disturbance in the child.

- A parent who systematically programs a child into a state of ongoing denigration and rejection of a loving and devoted parent is exhibiting complete disregard of the alienated parent's role in the child's upbringing. Such an alienating parent is bringing about a disruption of a psychological bond that could, in the vast majority of cases, prove of great value to the child--the separated and divorced status of the parents notwithstanding.

- Such alienating parents exhibit a serious parenting deficit, a deficit that should be given serious consideration by courts when deciding primary custodial status. Physical and/or sexual abuse of a child would quickly be viewed by the court as a reason for assigning primary custody to the nonabusing parent. Emotional abuse is much more difficult to assess objectively, especially because many forms of emotional abuse are subtle and difficult to verify in a court of law. The PAS, however, is most often readily identified, and courts would do well to consider its presence a manifestation of emotional abuse by the programming parent.

- Garbarino and Stott (1992) consider the PAS to be an example of what they refer to as "the psychologically battered child" and describe it specifically, by name, as one form of child battering. Rogers (1992) identifies five types of psychological maltreatment: rejecting, terrorizing, ignoring, isolating, and corrupting, and then describes how each of these types may be seen in the PAS. Accordingly, courts do well to consider the PAS programming parent to be exhibiting a serious parental deficit when weighing the pros and cons of custodial transfer. I am not suggesting that a PAS-inducing parent should automatically be deprived of primary custody, only that such induction should be considered a serious deficit in parenting capacity---a form of emotional abuse--and that it be given serious consideration when weighing the custody decision. (htt1)

Citation Page

http://www.alienationhurts.org/WhatIsParentalAlienation.htm

http://www.divorcesource.com/info/alienation/types.shtml

http://family-law.lawyers.com/visitation-rights/Parental-Alienation-Syndrome.html http://www.parental-alienation-awareness.com/

An Excellent Source of Additional Information:

www.parentalalienationawareness.org

www.AlienationHurts.org

www.squidoo.com/parental-alienation-syndrome-PAS

www.LeeP.A.S.Foundation.org